THIS JOURNAL BELONGS TO

....

Published in the United States by:
Hay House, Inc.: www.hayhouse.com®

Published in Australia by:
Hay House Australia Pty. Ltd.: www.hayhouse.com.au

Published in the United Kingdom by:
Hay House UK, Ltd.: www.hayhouse.co.uk

Published in India by:
Hay House Publishers India: www.hayhouse.co.in

Cover & interior design: Ashley Prine, Tandem Books
Cover illustration: © Claire Bremner
Image credits: Shutterstock: Back cover & interior decorative elements used throughout © Romanova Ekaterina; 11, 27, 67 © Elinorka; 31 © Amovitania (central image); 31 (crystals on top and bottom) © Tatiana Goncharuk; 37, 85 © Ladika888; 42 © Tata.Ya; 43 © Kusumayana KST; 54, 66 © Foxyliam; 55 © Olesia Agudova; 75 © Helen Lane; 79 © Viktorija Reuta; 87 © Tanya Leanovich; 93 (torso) © kichikimi; 93 (hand) © Viktoriia_M; 109 © Snowman200803; 115 © Aleksandr Gladkiy; 119 © Skye Creative Studio

Tradepaper ISBN: 978-1-4019-6864-9

10 9 8 7 6 5 4 3 2 1

1st edition, August 2022

Printed in the United States of America

EVENING
MEDITATIONS
Journal

RELAXING REFLECTIONS &
AFFIRMATIONS TO END YOUR DAY

The Hay House Editors

HAY HOUSE, INC.
Carlsbad, California • New York City
London • Sydney • New Delhi

INTRODUCTION

GOOD EVENING!

And welcome to your new nightly practice of meditation and journaling!

This journal is designed to be your personal companion for deepening your meditation experience. Whether you're new to meditation, familiar with it and looking to build a more regular practice, or already meditating regularly and want to explore and expand your repertoire, this journal will guide you to an evening routine that is tailored to your own preferences and interests.

Over the years, and indeed centuries, meditation has proven itself time and again as a beautifully beneficial practice for the body, mind, and soul. Modern studies continue to demonstrate what people have long intuited: meditation helps manage stress, increase your powers of concentration and memory, make you more creative, crystallize your sense of purpose, and improve your overall well-being. Evening is an especially effective time to meditate, because it gives you an opportunity to reflect on and unwind from your day. Evening meditation acts as the transition from the busyness and doing-going-acting of the day to the relaxing, recuperative, and rejuvenating downtime we all need.

While everyone can benefit from meditation, there's not a one-size-fits-all practice. There are lots of different ways to meditate, from the classic practice of sitting in silence to the alternate method of turning everyday activities into meditative moments.

This journal invites you to explore what's out there to find what suits you best. Writing about your meditation experiences helps you become mindful of what you like, what works for you, and how you're benefiting from your practice. It also can keep you motivated and coming back to sit every day.

On these pages, you'll find exercises to help you build your evening meditation practice by creating the time and space you need to realistically fit it into your schedule and household. You'll explore meditations to awaken your insight, heal your spirit, relax after a stressful day, let go of worry, build gratitude, live mindfully, create resonant mantras and affirmations, and achieve so much more. Guided prompts will introduce you to practices such as movement and object meditation, visualization, mindfulness, and tapping. You'll also find info on meditation companions like crystals, essential oils, herbs, and chakras so you can see if you like bringing them into your practice.

Journaling about these different ways of meditating as you try them will deepen the experience and allow you to build a lasting practice that you'll look forward to every evening. With plenty of space to write and even doodle and color, these meditations help you enjoy each and every evening so you can live more mindfully, gratefully, and intentionally. Namaste!

A *GOOD* EVENING MEDITATION

$\mathcal{S}$itting down to collect your thoughts and meditate at the end of the day can be a transformative practice. It helps you transition from the bustle and busyness of the day into the peace and calm of the evening, put down your to-do list, and acknowledge that you did your best today and now is the time to focus inward. Instead of racing through your day and then bringing that energy into your evening, mindfully step through the doorway of day into night, giving yourself the space you need to balance your time between work and rest. Stress less, sleep more, and foster positivity—now that's a *good* evening!

Think about what you want from your evening meditation practice. What would you like it to look like, and how do you want to feel afterward? Free yourself from any preconceived ideas of what it should be, and write about what a good evening meditation practice could mean for you.

....

....

....

....

....

....

"MY THOUGHTS
ARE AFFIRMATIONS
THAT SUPPORT THE
CREATION OF THE
REALITY I DESIRE."

–Iyanla Vanzant

YOUR THOUGHTS CREATE YOUR WORLD

*Y*our reality is, in so many ways, the product of your thoughts, of what you tell yourself. The way you perceive things, the way you feel about things, what you choose to do and not do are all rooted in your self-talk. Each thought you choose, even the negative ones, is an *affirmation* of what you want to see in your reality. So make sure to choose positive thoughts that reflect what you want to see in your reality. You are capable of so much when you tell yourself you can do something, when you know it to be true. Positive thinking is like a superpower!

What are some things you believed you could do and then did?

....

....

....

....

....

....

....

continued . . .

This evening, think of something you'd like to do but have told yourself isn't possible. Meditate on believing it can happen. How could you do it? How would it feel to accomplish it?

ZEN OUT COLORING

MAKE SPACE, LITERALLY

By making time to meditate in the evening, you're showing yourself love and care, which can be really helpful for winding down from the work of the day. If you want evening meditation to become a habit, try to make it as easy as possible for yourself. This means having a dedicated space for your practice. This doesn't mean you need a spotless, white room with a single cushion in the center whose sole purpose is meditation. It just needs to be a place where you feel comfortable and secure and can meditate undisturbed. You may choose to meditate in the traditional full- or half-lotus position, seated on a cushion on the floor with one or both feet resting on top of the thighs. Or you can sit upright in a comfy chair or spot on the couch with your feet on the floor. You might even decide you like to meditate lying down in bed. The important thing is to pick a place and position that are just right for you.

What would you like from your meditation space? How would you like to feel when you are there?

....

....

....

....

....

Sketch a picture of your ideal meditation spot. It can be a real space or somewhere fantastical. Let your mind run with it!

EVENING RITUAL

In addition to creating a space for yourself to meditate, you might consider making your meditation into a daily ritual. A simple ritual includes any set of actions you do to begin and end your practice—basically telling your brain to shift gears. By acknowledging the time as sacred and building a set of repeating actions around it, you are elevating the practice and infusing it with meaning.

You can choose any actions to be part of your ritual, as long as they feel special *to you*. For example, you might begin by lighting incense or diffusing some essential oil, putting on music or a relaxing soundscape, going through a light stretching or self-massage routine, speaking a specific mantra, or contacting a spirit guide. In this way, you'll be setting the intention and mood for the practice that follows. To end your practice, you'll want to choose something complementary to how you began it.

Describe how you see your ideal evening meditation ritual unfolding—how you feel, the actions you take, and the other healing practices you include.

....

....

....

....

MAKING TIME FOR EVENING MEDITATIONS

Setting aside time for evening meditations is an important part of building a practice. It can often be tempting to keep going with the tasks of the day or start on things you need to do at night and skip meditating in favor of these "more important" tasks. The truth is, though, nothing is more important than caring for yourself. Self-care and rest are the basis of anything else in your life. And if meditation is part of your self-care, making time for your practice should be a top priority. That may sound like a lot, but really you just need 10 or 15 minutes and a commitment to yourself. Here are some easy ways to make sure you get that time:

Set the scene. At some point during the day, give the place you meditate a once-over. Clean it of clutter, fluff up your cushions, and maybe even give it a little spritz of essential oil to make it a welcoming space that you can enter in the evening with no muss or fuss.

Plan ahead. Before you go to sit, decide what meditation you're going to do. That might mean selecting one from this journal, choosing one online or on an app, knowing the mantra or affirmation on which you'd like to meditate, or using any other method that you enjoy.

Gather what you need. Bring whatever you'll need for the meditation to the spot you plan to sit. If the meditation involves a writing exercise, or you like to journal before or after you sit, place your journal and pen or pencil there. If you want to incorporate a crystal or another item for an object meditation, have that easily at hand so you don't have to go hunting for it.

Set a time. Consistency is key for creating a practice, so if possible, try to meditate at about the same time each night. Find a spot in your usual evening routine. This might mean cutting back on some screen time, but the trade-off is well worth it.

Let the house know. Explain to those you live with that your evening meditation practice is important to you, and ask that they give you this time to yourself as an expression of their love and appreciation for you.

Reflect on why meditation is important to you, and write a commitment to yourself to practice it regularly. Decide when in your evening you can make the time for it.

....

....

....

....

....

....

....

....

BRAIN DUMP

Sometimes at the end of the day, your mind wants to keep going over and over what happened that day and what you need to do tomorrow. Maybe it's good stuff, maybe it's bad, maybe it's just a lot, but whatever it is, you're still chasing it around in your head instead of settling into the present. One of the easiest and most effective ways to clear your mind is to do a brain dump: sit down and write down whatever thoughts are coursing through your brain. Don't try to make them a story, and don't try to prioritize them or analyze. Just dump them out like you're turning a purse over and letting all that clutter inside stream out. You'll likely feel a lot lighter once you do.

Clear your mind by writing a stream-of-consciousness brain dump.

....

....

....

....

....

....

CHANGE YOUR MIND

How do you feel this evening? How do you usually feel when you end your day? Take some time to meditate on the thoughts and feelings you have today and those you commonly experience in the evening. Write about them below.

....

....

....

....

....

....

....

....

....

....

....

Now reflect on how you'd like to feel in the evenings. What thought patterns or habits could you change to point you in the right direction? If you wish, think of an affirmation or mantra you can say to yourself when you notice a thought or habit cropping up that you'd like to change.

....

....

....

....

....

....

....

....

....

....

END YOUR DAY ON A HIGH NOTE

"I did my best today."

"I am enough."

"I gave and received love today."

"Today I got to use my amazing body, mind, and soul."

Meditating on positive thoughts at the end of the day can cause a major shift in your overall attitude. By focusing on the good, the love, the abundance you have or want to attract, or anything else you like, you can deepen your recognition and appreciation of those things and draw more of them to you.

What positivity would you like to focus on at the end of the day? Freely write about it below.

....

....

....

....

....

....

....

"AFFIRMATIVE STATEMENTS ARE GOING BEYOND THE REALITY OF THE PRESENT INTO THE CREATION OF THE FUTURE THROUGH THE WORDS YOU USE IN THE NOW."

–Louise Hay

AFFIRM THE GOOD

Positive affirmations are short statements you repeat to yourself to help you consciously choose thoughts that will manifest your intended reality. Remember that whatever your mind is focused on, whether positive or negative, is what you'll see more of in your life. Many people say affirmations to themselves throughout their day, and your evening meditation practice is also a wonderful time to incorporate them.

What are your thoughts usually like at the end of the day: Are they negative, stress-filled, and focused on what you don't want? Or are they uplifting, positive, and focused on the good in life? Write about them here.

....

....

....

....

....

....

....

continued . . .

Create your own affirmations as a way of choosing empowering beliefs that build the foundation of your reality. For example, you might say "I am prosperous," even when there's little money in your bank account. Each time you think or say your affirmation, it builds that belief and attracts your future prosperity. Remember to always say affirmations in the present tense: statements in the future tense draw the energy toward that future time, so it never manifests in the now.

What are some positive affirmations you would like to meditate on at the end of the day? Write your affirmations down here. You can look at the affirmations on the next page for inspiration.

....

....

....

....

....

....

....

....

ZEN OUT COLORING

"All of the changes that lie before me are positive ones. I am safe."

"All is well in my world."

"I am beautiful, and everybody loves me."

"I am thankful for all the love in my life. I find it everywhere."

OBJECT MEDITATION

*O*ften when we meditate, we center our attention on the breath, sounds, or other sensations in the body to keep the mind focused and present, but there are so many things you can choose as your focal point. Find a small, beloved object. One that brings you joy. Get into a comfortable position, close your eyes, and meditate on this object with your hands. Feel its details, its texture, its increasing warmth from your hands. Make it the focus of your attention, reflecting on either the feel of the object or its meaning to you, whichever holds your attention best.

Draw your chosen object below and surround it with the words you associate with it.

DOODLE YOUR DAY

Let your creativity flow freely this evening! Maybe you want to illustrate your day, or maybe you just feel like making shapes or patterns. Doodle to your heart's content below, filling the page with anything you feel drawn to this evening.

GOOD NIGHT CRYSTALS

Crystals each have their own energy, their own vibration. Some are good listeners, absorbing the energy you put into them (I'm looking at you, clear quartz), while others are packed with healing energy. By adding crystals to your evening meditation practice, you can reflect on your day, heal from any hurts you experienced, or just wind down for a relaxing night. Here are some crystals you can try:

Ambronite can soothe you by dissolving anger and anxiety, bringing about relaxation and joy.

Amethyst promotes deeper meditation, especially when you're doing a visualization practice.

Blue calcite is a calming crystal that can help turn down the volume of racing thoughts and direct you to a higher level of contemplation.

Emerald can help calm your emotions and stabilize your mood.

Fluorite offers protection from negative energy and helps you reflect on situations so you can discern if they're having a positive or negative effect on you.

While different crystals do have specific energies, it's a good idea to let your intuition guide you to your crystals. If you open yourself up to that intuition, it can feel as if the crystals choose you! When you first bring a new crystal into your practice, you should cleanse it of any energy it's picked up from people along its way to you. There are many different clearing methods, but we recommend one of the following: passing it through smoke, letting it sit on a windowsill to absorb sun and moonlight for 24 hours, or pouring fresh water over it.

CRYSTALLIZE YOUR DAY

You can bring crystals into your evening meditation in a few ways. You can lie down and place crystals on any or all of your chakra points (see page 42), you can use them as the focus of an object meditation (see page 28), you can sit and hold crystals in your hand, or you can arrange them around you. Whatever way you choose to do it, meditate on the energy of each crystal, imagining its energy absorbing into you and coursing through your body, driving negativity out. Light in, dark out. If you have a certain part of your day that you'd like to heal or absorb, bring that visualization into your meditation.

How did you choose to do this meditation? Draw the orientation of your crystals below, and then write about how you felt during and after the meditation.

"THROUGH FOCUSING
THE MIND AND EXERCISING
THE BODY AND BREATH
IN SPECIFIC WAYS, WE
CAN ACTUALLY RELEASE
THE HABITUAL PATTERNS
OF THE CONCEPTUAL
MIND AND, AS A RESULT,
DIRECTLY DISCOVER
BEING."

–Tenzin Wangyal Rinpoche

MOVEMENT MEDITATION

*B*ringing movement into your evening meditation is a great way to release the day, as it allows you to channel any tension, preoccupied thoughts, or stress that you may still be experiencing and send it out of your body. Here is one way to do a movement meditation:

Stand up tall with your feet a little more than hip width apart. Inhale as you draw your hands up toward your chest and hold them together in prayer hands. Exhale as you bring your hands down and gently bend your knees. Repeat this movement with breath a few times and then start to sway with it, moving side to side as you rise with the inhale and root down with your exhales. Connect your breath to the movement and allow it to flow. Imagine any negative thoughts or feelings that you have being drawn into your lungs with your inhales and released with your exhales. There is no right way to do this, only what's right for you.

After your movement meditation, scan your body to see if you notice any sensations, like a tingling in the hands or relaxation in your muscles. Draw or write what you feel below.

continued . . .

*

How did the movement meditation affect your thoughts, your state of mind? How does the connection between your mind and body feel? Is it stronger perhaps?

....

....

....

....

....

....

....

....

....

....

....

ZEN OUT COLORING

MAKE ROUTINES INTO RITUALS

From the time we wake up to when we wind down in the evening, often we go through many of the same motions every day: cooking, washing dishes, drinking water, sweeping the floor. We may think of these things as chores or perhaps we don't think of them at all, but with a small shift in thinking, you can make these everyday practices into meditative rituals.

List some things that you do so often you do them by rote. Write down a couple of details about the actual motions and sensations of performing these acts. The sound of water running, the rhythm of the broom swishing, the satisfaction of finishing a task. Then, the next time you perform one of these daily "chores," focus on it. Meditate on it as self-care, as life itself. Try to really be present for it.

....

....

....

....

....

....

How did being meditative and present for your routine activities feel? Which ones do you think you may turn into rituals?

....

....

....

....

....

....

....

....

....

....

....

WALK OFF INTO THE SUNSET

An evening stroll at sunset is like walking into a little miracle. You can't help but be meditative as you watch the life-giving orb of light dip below the horizon, painting the sky with gorgeous strokes of color subtly shifting. It's truly a wonder to behold. Try a sunset walk and meditate on this everyday spectacle. Allow yourself to become immersed in the sky, the sounds, and the smells around you.

Write about what you felt, saw, heard, and smelled on your walk. Describe the emotions that came up as you meditated on the sunset.

....

....

....

....

....

....

....

THE CHAKRAS

The chakras are energy centers in your body. When all is well, they spin freely clockwise and allow energy to flow completely through you. While there are thought to be as many 78,000 chakras in the body, there are 7 major ones:

 The crown chakra is your higher consciousness and is associated with your spirituality and the universe.

 The third-eye chakra is linked to intuition, imagination, and psychic abilities.

 The throat chakra relates to communication, creativity, and your truth.

 The heart chakra is filled with compassion and love.

 The solar plexus chakra is concerned with willpowerand intellect.

 The sacral chakra is connected to emotions, sexuality, and creation.

 The root chakra (aka the base chakra) connects to the earth and embodies the survival instinct.

If one or more of these chakras are blocked, spinning counterclockwise, or overactive, it can throw off your whole system, making you feel sluggish, overwhelmed, or a whole host of other negative things. Meditation can help reopen chakras and get them spinning in the right direction.

THE CHAKRAS

The chakras are energy centers in your body. When all is well, they spin freely clockwise and allow energy to flow completely through you. While there are thought to be as many 78,000 chakras in the body, there are 7 major ones:

 The crown chakra is your higher consciousness and is associated with your spirituality and the universe.

 The third-eye chakra is linked to intuition, imagination, and psychic abilities.

 The throat chakra relates to communication, creativity, and your truth.

 The heart chakra is filled with compassion and love.

 The solar plexus chakra is concerned with willpowerand intellect.

 The sacral chakra is connected to emotions, sexuality, and creation.

 The root chakra (aka the base chakra) connects to the earth and embodies the survival instinct.

If one or more of these chakras are blocked, spinning counterclockwise, or overactive, it can throw off your whole system, making you feel sluggish, overwhelmed, or a whole host of other negative things. Meditation can help reopen chakras and get them spinning in the right direction.

A CHAKRA MEDITATION FOR THE EVENING

When your chakras are completely opened and spinning optimally, you feel at peace with yourself and the world around you. Use this meditation on those evenings when you're feeling a little off to bring you back to equilibrium.

Get into your favorite meditation pose. Close your eyes and bring your attention to your breath. Imagine a red, warming light forming at your root chakra and spreading out through your pelvis and legs. Picture that light rising up and becoming orange as it enters your sacral chakra and continuing up, turning yellow at your solar plexus, green at your heart, blue at your throat, and indigo at your third eye. Then imagine white light beaming from the top of your head, opening up an energetic connection between you and the universe.

How did this meditation feel? Did you feel like you could sense your chakras? Did you notice any difficult areas or blockages?

....

....

....

....

....

AN EVENING OF HEALING

If you've been feeling stressed or unwell, try taking an evening to meditate on healing. Start by putting on some calming music, getting into a comfortable position, and closing your eyes. Breathe in slowly through your nose and exhale through your mouth. Allow yourself to get into a rhythm with this. Then check in with your body. Imagine a white light traveling around each part, scanning for tension or injury. When you come to a place that you feel needs healing or release, breathe healing energy into it with five deep breaths. With each breath, the white light gets brighter and brighter.

How do you feel after this meditation? What areas felt like they needed healing? How do they feel now?

....

....

....

....

....

....

BREATHE IN CALM

*S*ettle into your favorite meditation position and begin to focus on your breathing. As you inhale, feel the soothing rush of air fill you up, inflating you, making you light. As you exhale, breathe out any heaviness or tension that built up in you over the course of the day. With each breath, feel yourself becoming lighter and lighter until you fill up like a balloon and start to float. Imagine yourself drifting around on a calm breeze. Continue until you feel ready to come back down to the ground.

On a scale of 1 to 10, how calm do you feel now? How did your feelings of tension or calm change over the course of the meditation?

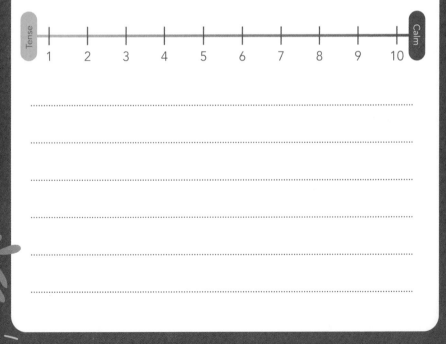

Tense
1   2   3   4   5   6   7   8   9   10
Calm

Draw the scene you imagined as you were a balloon floating on the breeze.

"WHEN WE REALLY START
TO TUNE IN TO WHO LIFE
INTENDED US TO BE—
AND WE'RE ATTUNED
TO THE EMOTIONS THAT
MOTIVATE US—WE
CONNECT WITH THE SOUL
OF OUR MAGNIFICENCE."

–Anita Moorjani

LISTEN TO YOURSELF

Cultivate your relationship with yourself this evening by listening for your true inner guidance during your meditation.

What did you hear?

....

....

....

....

....

....

....

....

....

....

SUNSET YOUR WORRY

Sometimes it's hard to let go of a worry, especially when it's over something you know you'll have to do or face in the near future. But taking a break from your stressors is key not only to handling them but to protecting your mental and physical health as well. This meditation can help you put away a worry so you can have a restful and restorative night and face the world fresh tomorrow. Start by identifying your source of stress as clearly as you can.

What are you worried about?

....

....

....

....

....

....

....

....

Now that you have a clear sense of your worry, you can more effectively let it go for the night. Get into your favorite meditation position and bring your attention to your breath. Once you are settled in, picture a bright, clear day with the sun high in the sky. Take whatever worry you have and imagine it being eclipsed by the sun, enveloped in the white, healing light of our nearest star. Now watch as the sun begins to drop in the sky, toward the horizon. The colors of the sky warm into yellow, orange, and red. Then the colors cool to pink, purple, and indigo as the sun slowly sinks out of sight. Sit here for as long as you like, watching the stars come out.

What emotions or thoughts came up during your meditation? How are you feeling now?

....

....

....

....

....

....

....

GOOD EVENING HERBS

There's nothing quite like a soothing cup of herbal tea to relax you at the end of the day. Some herbs are good for releasing tension, others aid in muscle relaxation, and then there are herbs that can help you sleep. Here are a few you might consider adding to your evening routine:

 Chamomile is the classic go-to tea for getting sleepy. It's been used for centuries to calm tension and anxiety to help people sleep, and it also helps with digestion.

 Hawthorn reduces nervousness and tension and even acts as a very mild sedative, making it useful on nights when you're feeling wound up.

 Holy basil is beloved in Ayurvedic medicine for its abilities to lift your mood while relaxing you at the same time.

 Lemon balm can reduce anxiety, soothe a nervous stomach, and help calm you down when you feel overwhelmed.

 Valerian has been used since Greek and Roman times. It is believed to have a sedative effect that can soothe anxiety and help people fall asleep faster.

NIGHT-TEA NIGHT

The simple act of brewing a cup of tea and sipping it slowly in your favorite comfy spot can be a wonderfully relaxing and meditative experience at the end of the day. Being mindful of each part of the process can enhance the experience and its benefits. Pay attention to the sounds of the water filling the kettle and coming to a bubbly boil, the warm waft of the steam rushing up from the mug as you fill it, the soothing aroma of the tea. Then, as you sit, enjoy the time it takes for the tea to cool off enough to drink, then savor each sip as a moment full of healing and ease.

As you sip your tea, write here, in a stream-of-consciousness way. Allow yourself the freedom to write whatever you like, just for the joy of writing it.

....

....

....

....

....

....

....

"GIVING THANKS, RECOGNIZING ALL THE GOOD IN YOUR LIFE, IS THE GATEWAY DRUG TO A LIFE MOST EXTRAORDINARY. IT'S THE SUPERPOWER THAT MOVES YOU ONTO THE FREQUENCY WHERE BEAUTY AND JOY AND CREATIVITY HAPPEN."

–Pam Grout

WHAT A GREAT DAY!

_T_oday was great! That simple thought can be a revolution. If each day you focus on all that you're blessed with, all the good that happened, and all that is right in your world, instead of letting your thoughts continuously beat the drum of what you need or what went wrong, your life will transform into one of beauty and wonder. It's a simple, powerful idea, but it takes work if you're like most people and used to thinking about the negative instead of the positive.

List everything you're grateful for from your day, from the big to the small. Do your best to fill up every line.

....

....

....

....

....

....

....

....

continued . . .

Now think of all those things that you don't have yet, but that you want to bring into your reality. Write them here as affirmations, expressing gratitude for each one as if it has already come to pass.

....

....

....

....

....

....

....

....

....

....

....

ARE YOU FREE THIS EVENING?

Most meditations aim to focus the mind on something, whether it be your breath, a mantra, or clearing the mind of thought as much as possible. This meditation is just the opposite. Instead of trying to hone a sense of control or focus, give yourself permission to set aside all that effort of taming your "monkey mind," as it's known. Settle into your favorite meditation with your eyes opened or closed and just be. Let your thoughts run free without judging them. Don't try to focus on them or control them. Sit for as long as you like and just watch the show.

What did you notice about your thoughts during this free-form meditation?

....

....

....

....

....

....

....

ABUNDANCE AFFIRMATIONS

"I accept and receive abundance."
"I attract abundance."
"I am worthy of abundance."

Love, wealth, health, safety, happiness—we all deserve these things in abundance! To attract abundance in all things, you have to believe you deserve it; you have to believe having all you desire is possible and *good*. Meditating on an affirmation is a powerful method for attracting abundance, but only if the affirmation rings true for you. That is why it is important to choose affirmations carefully, change them to suit your own voice, or even write your own.

Explore what abundance means to you and what you are looking to attract. Write about this with some detail, then distill from that longer journal entry a brief affirmation that resonates with you down to your core.

....

....

....

....

....

....

EASE YOUR MIND WITH ESSENTIAL OILS

Adding a scent-scape to your evening meditation practice can be used to create a relaxing ritual you'll look forward to each day. There are many lovely oils that not only smell great, but also help you unwind and calm a racing mind. Here are a few essential oils that can contribute to a peaceful night:

Frankincense has a deep spicy, earthy smell that is thought to relieve anxiety and put you in a meditative state.

Lavender is well known for its calming aroma. It can also ease muscle tension, nervousness, and even an upset stomach.

Lemongrass promotes relaxation and can help you recover from anxiety more quickly.

Neroli is believed to reduce anxiety and help stop or lessen worried thoughts.

Ylang-ylang can help you de-stress, and it may also lower your blood pressure.

SMELL THAT NIGHT AIR

Bringing aromatherapy into a meditation not only adds the health benefit of the chosen herb to your practice but it can also help ground your mind and focus your thoughts. For this meditation, choose a calming herb and use whatever delivery method you like: you can diffuse essential oils, apply skin-safe oils to your skin (be sure to dilute with a carrier oil), burn incense or a candle, or spritz a room spray.

Now settle into your favorite meditation posture. Close your eyes and bring your attention to your breath. Inhale slowly through your nose, sending the aroma of the herb into your nostrils. Notice the smell; pay attention to how the air feels as it travels into your sinuses, down your throat, and into your lungs. Imagine its calming properties suffusing your system, circulating through your body. Make the aroma the focus of your attention. When your thoughts wander, bring them back to the scent. Sit for as long as you like.

How do you feel after your meditation? What effect did the aromatherapy have?

....

....

....

....

....

WATER WORKS

A warm bath or shower in the evening is a wonderful opportunity for a relaxing sensory meditation. Light some candles or get out a fancy soap or bath bomb you've been saving and go into the water with self-care in mind. Incorporate incense or essential oils for some aromatherapy. Take in the cleansing scents, feel the slippery textures, watch the iridescent bubbles form and pop on your skin, and feel any stress from the day slip away. If any worries or stressors start to break through, refocus on your breath and gently bring your mind back to what you feel.

Describe your experience and how you feel now, after your meditative self-care cleanse.

....

....

....

....

....

....

....

"MINDFULNESS BEGINS
WHEN WE MOVE FROM
A MODE OF DOING
AND THINKING, AND
INTO A WAY OF BEING,
WHERE SENSING TAKES
CENTER STAGE."

–Dr. Ed Halliwell

A GROUNDING
MINDFULNESS MEDITATION

*B*ringing your awareness to your surroundings through your senses, instead of focusing so much on your thoughts, is the heart of mindfulness, which in itself is a kind of meditation. And coming into a grounded, mindful state in the evening helps you transition from the work of the day to a restorative night. This simple technique will help land you in your evening so you can fully appreciate this time of rest.

List five things that you see.

....

....

....

....

....

List four things that you feel.

....

....

....

continued . . .

List three things that you hear.

....

....

....

List two things that you smell.

....

....

List one thing that you taste.

....

How do you feel? What sense do you feel most connected to?

....

....

....

....

....

....

ZEN OUT COLORING

SEE YOURSELF

It's easy to get caught up in doing things and lose sight of *how you're doing*. Meditate on these self-awareness questions to check in with yourself and gain some insight into you.

List the five most important things in your life.

....

....

....

....

....

What are your best qualities?

....

....

....

....

....

....

What are your dreams or goals?

....

....

....

....

....

How are you going (or how could you go) after your dreams?

....

....

....

....

....

....

FEEL YOURSELF

You may hold tension or stress in your body without even realizing you're doing it, perhaps until it causes a physical problem. Doing a relaxing body scan can help you find spots where you're bracing or straining and release that stress.

Start by lying down in a comfortable position. Take a few deep breaths to settle in. Then bring your awareness to your feet. Mentally scan your toes, your arches, the top of your feet, the bones and muscles inside. If you notice a spot that is tense or painful, keep your attention and breathe into that spot. Imagine that breath carrying healing to the spot, as the tension releases. Notice any thoughts or emotions that come up as you breathe into the spot.

Once you've done your feet, move your attention up through your whole body. Go slowly and scan each and every part.

How do you feel now?

Where did you feel tension? Mark the spots below and write down any thoughts or emotions that came up for them.

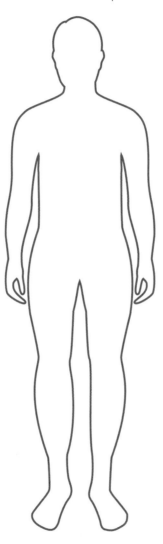

ACCEPT YOURSELF

We can all be hard on ourselves, especially when the day hasn't gone our way. But learning to accept the parts of yourself you might see as shortcomings or flaws is one of the greatest acts of self-care you can undertake.

This evening, spend some time meditating on you. Think of something about yourself that you've always thought was a negative and write a letter to yourself accepting that part of you as one bit of the beautiful whole. See if you can recast it in a positive light and give it a little love.

"TRUE SELF-LOVE IS WHEN YOU APPRECIATE WHERE YOU ARE AND WHO YOU ARE, REGARDLESS OF ANY TRANSFORMATION YOU ASPIRE TO."

–Vex King

LOVE YOURSELF

A lot of times it's easy to love others but forget to extend that same loving feeling to yourself. Meditating on self-love creates space in your heart for you, which can be a wonderful means of self-discovery and healing.

This evening, foster some love for yourself by getting into your favorite meditation position and placing one hand on your heart. As you breathe, try to feel the beat of your heart. Focus on the subtle feelings of your breath and heartbeat—your life rhythm. Now imagine a warm red, loving light emanating from your hand. Really feel the love and allow it to spread through your body, until your whole being is aglow with self-love. Keep with this meditation as long as you like.

After the meditation, list all your awesome traits. They can be things you're good at, things you've accomplished, and the quirks that make you you.

....

....

....

....

....

....

continued . . .

ZEN OUT COLORING

A SIMPLE MANTRA

Mantras are verbal tools that concentrate your thoughts, like a magnifying glass focusing the diffused light of the sun into a powerful beam. Repeating a mantra aloud and with rhythm can help put you into a deep meditative state that reduces stress levels and can bring about a feeling of well-being or even elation.

The single syllable *om* is believed to connect one to the self as well as the ultimate reality and has been used as a mantra for thousands of years. This evening, try repeating om (pronounced "aum") as you meditate. Inhale gently through the nose and then allow the sound of om to emanate from deep within you on each long outbreath.

How did meditating using the om mantra make you feel? How was it different from a silent meditation?

....

....

....

....

....

....

COUNT TO CALM

This simple meditation can be done in the evening to help land you in the relaxing part of your day. First, check in with yourself.

How calm or stressed do you feel?

Get into your favorite meditation position and close your eyes. Take a steady breath in through your nose, down into your belly, and at the moment you shift to a slow exhale through your mouth, begin counting with "one." Repeat this up through ten and then back down again as many times as you like. Or, you could list the colors of the rainbow, from energetic red to calming blue and purple; recite the alphabet; write a list of things you're grateful for and then say them aloud—whatever feels familiar and calming.

You can do an abbreviated version of this meditation anytime you feel yourself getting worked up and want to calm down quickly. Just close your eyes wherever you are and count to calm.

Now how calm or stressed do you feel?

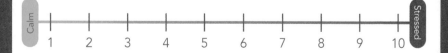

What did you "count"? Did you use numbers, colors, or something else? How did your feelings of calm or stress change from before to after your meditation?

A QUIET EVENING

As social creatures, we spend a lot of time talking with people, listening to podcasts or the radio, watching TV, and doing other activities that fill our minds with sounds. Happily chatting away and listening to your favorite music can absolutely fill your cup, but sometimes silence can help you really hear. This evening, take a mini silent retreat for the final few hours of the day. After dinner, resist the urge to speak or turn on the TV or radio, and ask the people in your home to keep as quiet as possible.

Take note of how you feel. Listen to your body and the deeper voice within. What can you hear in the silence?

....

....

....

....

....

....

....

PUT A GOOD EVENING ON TAP

Tapping, also known as EFT (emotional freedom technique), is a simple practice that clears blockages to rebalance the energy in your body and help you overcome limiting beliefs. It's like a very gentle form of self-acupressure. To start, identify something you'd like to change, your "most pressing issue." Let's say you want to decrease your anxiety.

Sum up the issue you'd like to work on, then express that you love and accept yourself, despite the issue. This is your "setup statement." For example: "Even though I feel anxious and overwhelmed, I deeply love and accept myself." Then come up with a shortened form of your setup statement: your "reminder phrase." With our example, you might say "This anxiety . . ." or "I'm anxious and overwhelmed . . ."

....

....

....

Next, take one or two fingers and tap on the side of your hand while saying your setup statement three times. Then assess how you feel.

....

....

....

The illustration below shows the eight points you'll be tapping on in sequence: eyebrow, side of eye, under eye, under nose, chin, collarbone, under arm, then top of head. Tap on each point several times, saying your reminder phrase out loud before moving on to the next point.

Once you've completed a cycle, assess how you feel. How does it compare to what you wrote earlier?

....

....

....

Continue tapping on the eight points in the sequence, if needed, until you feel the blocks around the issue beginning to clear.

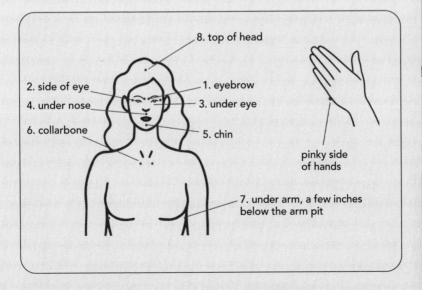

8. top of head

2. side of eye

4. under nose

6. collarbone

1. eyebrow

3. under eye

5. chin

pinky side of hands

7. under arm, a few inches below the arm pit

"WHEN YOU ARE ABLE
TO PASSIONATELY FEEL
WHATEVER IT IS THAT
YOU WISH TO HAVE OR
BECOME, AS LONG AS IT
IS ALIGNED WITH YOUR
HIGHEST SELF—THAT IS,
GOD—YOU BECOME IT
AND IT BECOMES YOU."

–Wayne W. Dyer

MAKE IT A GOOD EVENING

 $\mathcal{Y}$ ou can help turn your wishes and desires into reality through manifestation—the belief that your wishes and desires *will* be fulfilled. It's the feeling of utter positivity that an outcome will happen. And one of the most powerful tools for believing a wish will be realized is meditation.

First, be clear about what you want to manifest. Write below in detail what it is you want and how you will *get it.*

....

....

....

....

....

....

....

....

....

....

continued . . .

*Now write about any limiting beliefs you have about your wish.
These are the ways you tell yourself you won't get what you want.*

....

....

....

....

....

....

*Then go back and cross out all your limits! Or write over them with
positive messages. Do whatever you feel to show yourself you're
getting rid of those beliefs.*

....

....

....

....

....

....

Finally, come up with a manifestation affirmation to meditate on. Something like, "I am open to all the abundance the world has to offer me." Write some below until you come up with one that really resonates with you, then silently repeat it to yourself tonight as you meditate for 10 minutes or however long you like.

FIVE-MINUTE RULE

Sometimes you just don't wanna. You've had a long day and even though your meditation practice has been going strong, tonight you just don't feel like sitting. Rather than give in to this temptation and skip meditating, or force yourself to sit for a long time even if you aren't feeling it, try this nice middle road: a five-minute no rules meditation. Simply sit for five minutes with no agenda—that's it. Don't try to control your breath or your thoughts or your thoughts about your thoughts. Just let it all go for five minutes with no direction and no judgments, focusing on something like the breath only if you want to. Then get up and go treat yourself in a way that's meaningful for you. Or continue to sit.

What gets in your way when it comes to meditating?

....

....

....

....

....

....

MIND YOUR DINNER

*E*ating mindfully can be a meditative experience. Being aware of the rich aromas, the feel of the food in your hand and in your mouth, the wonderful flavors—it's a meal for the senses and your belly. When you eat dinner this evening, try to focus on the whole experience. The careful cooking, the experience of eating something so nourishing, the exchange of energy from the food to your body, the gratitude you feel for the food itself and its preparation—try to immerse yourself in it fully.

How was the experience? What are your feelings of gratitude toward your food like? If you have a prayer or other form of recognition you use to honor your food, write it below.

....

....

....

....

....

....

....

....

DREAM INCUBATION

By focusing on a question before you go to sleep, you can prompt your subconscious mind to release an answer that's been brewing deep in your thoughts but that you have yet to articulate. This practice is known as dream incubation, and people have explored it for millennia, from the ancient Egyptians to researchers at Massachusetts Institute of Technology. People have found it helpful for solving problems, preparing for a big event, or revisiting a great experience.

Say, for example, you have to give a presentation you're nervous about, or you're going to have a difficult conversation with someone. If you incubate a dream where things go really well, you'll likely be more confident and comfortable when the waking moment arrives. You may also do or say something brilliant in your dream that your waking mind hasn't come up with yet.

What question do you want to ask your dreams? Write freely about your question in as much detail as you can, then distill all of that down to a single question you can repeat to yourself as you fall asleep tonight. It's best to keep the question open-ended, something more like "What is my purpose in life?" than the more practical, yet harder to pinpoint, "What are the winning lottery numbers?"

GOOD EVENING VIBRATIONS

You and everyone and everything around you emit vibrations. You can feel them coming off people when you walk into a room or coming from nature when you're in a truly beautiful place. We are all in silent conversation with one another through vibrations, and the more you tune in to that, the more you can put out good vibes and pick up the vibes you want.

This evening, reflect on the vibes and beliefs you're putting out there and the ones you're taking in from those around you. Then write some affirmations to help you shape those vibes for whatever abundance you're looking for, whether that be health, wealth, safety, love, or peace.

"LIFE HAS AN ENERGY, A FEELING, A PROFOUND CONSCIOUSNESS, A FULLNESS, AND A DEEP, DEEP SENSE OF INNATE CONNECTION WITH ALL OTHER LIFE. THAT FEELING—THAT KNOWING—IS RIGHT HERE."

–Pedram Shojai, O.M.D.

LOVE CONNECTION

This evening, nourish yourself with love's powers of healing and connectivity! With this loving-kindness meditation, you'll also develop your sense of compassion for yourself and all others.

Start by writing a list of people you treasure and what you love about them. Then, get into your favorite meditation position, close your eyes, and settle down. Think about those people and allow yourself to really feel the love you have for them. Let that love fill your chest and lift the corners of your mouth into a smile. One by one, picture each person as clearly as you can and send that feeling of love out to them. (Don't worry about recalling everyone from your list—just allow people to come to your mind.) Once you've gone through specific people who come to mind, send that feeling of love out to your street, your town, and your state, then let it radiate out to the country and the world. Finally, send that really big love inward, to yourself.

Write down the names of people you treasure and then describe what you love about them.

....

....

....

....

....

continued . . .

ZEN OUT COLORING

COUNT YOUR BLESSINGS

Practicing gratitude is a panacea for the mind, spirit, and body. When you focus on all the things you have in your life that you're grateful for, you actively and specifically recognize how blessed you are. You shift your thoughts away from what you need to achieve, acquire, problem solve, or figure what's next to rooting them in this beautiful moment, where you are blessed with abundance and all is well.

Count your blessings below, then meditate on them. Take your time. Savor each blessing and the gratitude you feel toward it.

....

....

....

....

....

....

....

....

HUG THERAPY

Hugs feel great, but it turns out they're also really good for you! They can reduce stress, pain, and anxiety, release feel-good hormones in the body, and even lower blood pressure. And the longer the hug, the better. So this evening, find somebody and ask them to do some hug therapy with you!

Start by sitting and doing a short and simple meditation together. Just a few minutes of focusing on the breath is all you need. You may even choose to hold hands while you meditate to start a connection flowing. Then hug for at least 20 seconds.

How did it feel to meditate with someone in this way? Did you feel any shifts in your body or mind as you hugged?

....

....

....

....

....

....

....

FEED YOUR SPIRIT

Making time for the things you really love in this world is how you feed your spirit. These are the things that make you laugh, help you feel like you're in the flow of the universe, and bring you joy. They can be anything—cooking, volunteering, crafting, dancing, getting a massage, mountain climbing, yodeling, doing literally nothing. When we say anything, we mean it! And the more in tune you are with this kind of soul food, the better nourished you'll be.

If you feel guilty about focusing on yourself, remember that you cannot pour from an empty vessel. Filling your own cup first enables you to then serve others.

Spend some time meditating on what fills your cup. Then list what you came up with on this page, and keep writing or drawing on the next.

....

....

....

....

....

....

"THE SPIRIT WITHIN
YOU IS THE PRESENCE
OF INSPIRATION, JOY,
AND THE TRUTH OF
WHO YOU ARE."

–Gabrielle Bernstein

JOY MULTIPLICATION

*Y*esterday you meditated on the things that fill your cup, and this evening, you're going to dive deeper into that spiritual sustenance that inspires and feeds the true you.

Pick a few of the most fulfilling things you wrote or draw and list them here, but leave a few lines empty between each one. Then list the little things within those big things that bring you joy. If you love cooking, what are the little details that delight you? If you picked your dog, what makes your fur baby the best in the world? See how many factors of joy you can deduce from each big source of joy.

continued . . .

ZEN OUT COLORING

✳ ASK IN CONTEMPLATION

*S*itting in quiet contemplation of a question is a version of meditation we perhaps don't do as often as others. Typically we sit and meditate on breathing or feelings such as gratitude or calm, but meditation can also be a time when you sit and ponder the big questions, like What does it mean to be good? or What is the meaning of life? Unanswerable as they are, they are nonetheless important and satisfying to think about.

This evening, choose one of life's great mysteries and meditate on it. Write any insights that come to you.

....

....

....

....

....

....

....

....

....

WHAT YOU'VE LEARNED

Congratulations on completing this journal journey! You've explored all sorts of techniques and exercises for meditating, and hopefully you've learned some things about yourself along the way.

Tonight, flip through your entries in this journal to see what you've learned, what you've enjoyed, what you'd like to keep practicing, and what's not quite for you and write down your discoveries here.

....

....

....

....

....

....

....

....

Hay House Titles of Related Interest

The Gift of Gratitude: A Guided Journal for Counting Your Blessings,
by Louise Hay

The High 5 Daily Journal,
by Mel Robbins

Living Your Purpose Journal,
by Dr. Wayne W. Dyer

Morning Meditations Journal,
by The Hay House Editors

The Sacred Cycles Journal,
by Jill Pyle, Em Dewey, and Cidney Bachert

Sweet Dreams Journal,
by The Hay House Editors

Zen Meditations Journal,
by The Hay House Editors

All of the above are available at your local bookstore,
or may be ordered by contacting Hay House (see next page).

* * *

We hope you enjoyed this Hay House book. If you'd like to receive our online catalog featuring additional information on Hay House books and products, or if you'd like to find out more about the Hay Foundation, please contact:

Hay House, Inc., P.O. Box 5100, Carlsbad, CA 92018-5100
(760) 431-7695 or (800) 654-5126
(760) 431-6948 (fax) or (800) 650-5115 (fax)
www.hayhouse.com® • www.hayfoundation.org

———

Published in Australia by: Hay House Australia Pty. Ltd.,
18/36 Ralph St., Alexandria NSW 2015
Phone: 612-9669-4299 • *Fax:* 612-9669-4144
www.hayhouse.com.au

Published in the United Kingdom by: Hay House UK, Ltd.,
The Sixth Floor, Watson House, 54 Baker Street, London W1U 7BU
Phone: +44 (0)20 3927 7290 • *Fax:* +44 (0)20 3927 7291
www.hayhouse.co.uk

Published in India by: Hay House Publishers India,
Muskaan Complex, Plot No. 3, B-2, Vasant Kunj, New Delhi 110 070
Phone: 91-11-4176-1620 • *Fax:* 91-11-4176-1630
www.hayhouse.co.in

———

Access New Knowledge.
Anytime. Anywhere.

Learn and evolve at your own pace
with the world's leading experts.

www.hayhouseU.com

SOURCES

Page 8: *Get Over It!: Thought Therapy for Healing the Hard Stuff*, Iyanla Vanzant

Page 24: *I Can Do It: How to Use Affirmations to Change Your Life*, Louise Hay

Page 34: *Awakening the Sacred Body: Tibetan Yogas of Breath and Movement*, Tenzin Wangyal Rinpoche

Page 50: *Dying to Be Me: My Journey from Cancer, to Near Death, to True Healing*, Anita Moorjani

Page 58: *Thank & Grow Rich: A 30-Day Experiment in Shameless Gratitude and Unabashed Joy*, Pam Grout

Page 72: *Mindfulness: How to Live Well by Paying Attention*, Dr. Ed Halliwell

Page 82: *Good Vibes, Good Life: How Self-Love Is the Key to Unlocking Your Greatness*, Vex King

Page 94: *Wishes Fulfilled: Mastering the Art of Manifesting*, Wayne W. Dyer

Page 106: *Focus: Bringing Time, Energy, and Money into Flow*, Pedram Shojai, O.M.D.

Page 116: *Super Attractor: Methods for Manifesting a Life Beyond Your Wildest Dreams*, Gabrielle Bernstein